horizons

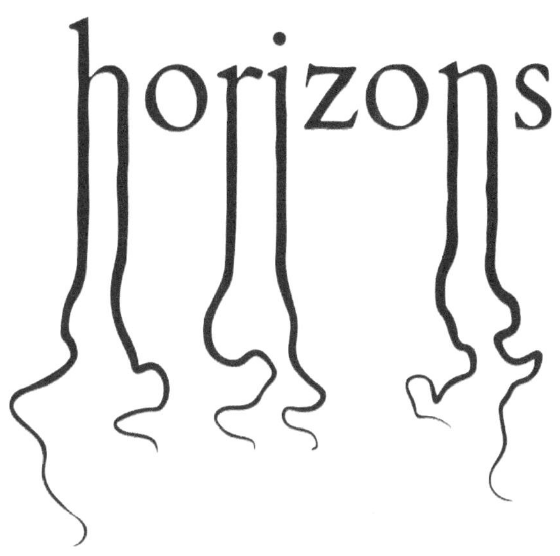

poetry by
Julie S. Paschold

atmosphere press

For my father, who taught me to broaden my horizons

and

for my mother, who taught me the words to share them with you.

Contents

Topsoil

Introduction

When the average person hears the word *horizon*, they probably think of looking out along the edge of the earth, gazing at a sunset or a sunrise, at the junction of earth and sky.

But ask any scientist who has studied how the earth forms, and they will know that soil also has horizons. A soil is divided into horizons, which look like layers. They are zones of differentiated weathering that occur when the environment encounters a sedimentary rock. Soil horizons represent some type of modification of the properties of this rock, what soil scientists call the parent material. The differing environmental factors combined with a variety of parent materials means that soils can have extreme variations, depending on where they are and how they were formed. Each soil has a different personality. Formation of a new soil is so slow that we must consider it nonrenewable in our time frame of a few hundred years. Soil is formally defined as *the layer(s) of generally loose mineral and/or organic material that are affected by physical, chemical, and/or biological processes at or near the planetary surface and usually hold liquids, gases, and biota and support plants* (CSA News). This is a cold way of defining the living, changing, interactive medium that lies underneath our feet.

Scientists label these horizons using the alphabet, starting with the top horizon, and moving towards the earth's core. The A horizon is the topsoil, the B horizon is the subsoil, and the parent material, the C horizon. The soil, however, develops in the opposite direction. It begins in the parent material (C horizon), develops some structure and becomes subsoil (the B horizon), then interacts more with the environment and organisms in its ecosystem, and becomes the topsoil (A horizon). A topsoil that has been worked by humans for farming, as an example, becomes an Ap horizon, or a plow layer.

My book *Horizons* is divided into three sections, three horizons, to honor this nonrenewable resource. To connect more closely with this resource, we shall travel with the soil, and start with the parent material, moving towards the surface and the sun.

We must be more cognizant of how the actions we take affect the very earth beneath us, and how soil supports all of us, not only the plants and their roots.

Dr. Dan

For Dr. Dan Walters and the University of Nebraska-Lincoln
Agronomy Department

Dr. Dan says dirt is a four-letter word.
Dirt is soil where you don't want it—
on the bottom of your shoes,
under your fingernails.
Here we use the word soil.

Dr. Dan says we need special boots
when we work in the field,
soil sampling with the hydraulic probe
attached to the back of the pickup
that can penetrate thirteen feet
into the ground,
the one he works with a cigarette
dangling from his mouth.
Go buy leather steel toe Red Wings
down at the shoe store in Havelock.

Dr. Dan says kids should be able
to play in the compost pile,
and brings his in buckets
on Saturdays for elementary school kids
to find earthworms and centipedes,
millipedes and a host of other critters
squiggling over their fingers.

Dr. Dan orders his work pickups
stripped down with only the essentials—
he even tries to get the radios removed—

so we can do our work
without distraction.
The oldest is a white 1976 Ford
on which I learn to drive stick shift
following a graduate student
from the field plots to the shed
while he brings the tractor back in.

Dr. Dan says there is a difference
between agronomy and soil science,
and makes sure I am schooled
in things both above and below ground.

Dr. Dan reminds me
it takes five rinses in clean water
to get the soap out of the lab glassware,
setting it to air dry
on the huge black counter tops
in his lab.

Dr. Dan, when he passes,
is lowered into the very soil
he studied all of his life.

Dr. Dan leaves a legacy
in the soil fertility project,
at the university,
in the minds of the students
he guided and left behind.

PARENT MATERIAL

Developing soil starts out in the parent material, also called the C horizon. Technically, this horizon contains the weathered material that came from the parent material and most resembles the original weathered rock. The C horizon is the lowest horizon that sits on top of the bedrock and has very little soil structure, if any. The original parent material can be rock that exists in the area below the C horizon, or could have been deposited in the area via air (like wind), water, ice (like glaciers), or volcanic ash.

This is the horizon that hasn't moved far from home. Family is important, and it follows closely in its parents' footsteps.

'68 International

My first memory of riding
in anything with wheels
is of sitting between my daddy
wearing a work-worn pocket tee
maneuvering the stick shift
I am to keep my tiny feet away from
and my twin sister
who is equally enthralled as I am
at the gravel road passing beneath us
visible through the rusted-out hole in the floor board
of our 1968 International pickup
the color red
faded now almost to orange
as my husband pulls it from the tree-line
where it slept for some decades
while my son and daughter
small enough to stand straight in the rim of a tractor's wheel
look on
and the great metal beast is hauled 100 miles north
shaking startled mice from its bowels upon parking
where it sits once more
waiting for the funds to mend
so I may be that little girl
safely riding beside the man I adore.

Mom

You've held my hand,
my words of doubt and fear and pain,
reshaped them into phrases
of hope and acceptance and comfort,
molded each trouble with
the palms of your guidance,
pressed sparkle into the
deepest pits of my depressions.
Who do you turn to
when your scars are too heavy
to burden alone?
Although I often seek solitude,
I will forever be reaching
for the embrace
of your lively, dancing,
luminous soul.

Arbor Day

To my twin sister

Do you remember when
we thought you were allergic
to the crab apple trees
at the top of the hill
at our grade school?
I was so mad at those trees
for being so beautiful.
Those delicate petals
falling so dramatically
yet so serenely to the grass below,
the flowers hugging their branches tightly
in hues of magenta, burgundy, and lilac
between creased pointed oval leaves
and smelling so sweetly.
I did not want the desire
to walk up that hill
and take each future fruit into my hands,
to talk to it gently,
to learn of the earth and the grass
and its creatures below
but there I was,
a plant lover and a critter lover
even then,
betraying my allergy-ridden other half
whispering *tell me*
tell me your secrets oh rooted one
and I will listen
with rapt attention
and eager eye.

Though my heart may scatter and scar
I will come back to both of you,
giver of life and keeper of soul.

I am here to listen again
so tell me
tell me and root me
dear tree
dear sister
tell me.

I Can See Clearly Now

that I've gone to the
ophthalmologist after two years
and bought new bright blue frames
with my updated prescription,

this being the seventh year
I've had to partake of bifocals,
my eyes gradually worsening
as the years progress,

but she could not see,
this small elderly woman
seated between my twin sister
and me at the piano bench,

my eight-year-old legs swinging
as she deftly picked out the notes
and the keys without sight,
having lost the ability at age sixteen,

now in her ninth decade of life,
playing music for her great-
grandchildren, awing us with
her ability to navigate her home
without use of her eyes,

her memory coming to mind
years later when I see an article
of an artist displaying pictures
in three dimensions,

a merging of photography and sculpture
to enable the blind to see the art,
her memory popping up here and there,

this sightless great-grandmother
with the ability to allow her progeny
to see the world in a different light,

a world that closed its eyes to her
when she was young,
a world that she could
not help
but care for.

For my mother's maternal grandmother, Esther Swartz Griess

Grandma's Hands

For my paternal grandmother, Aldyth Paschold

Grandma's hands
    could tell stories
    of when everything was homemade:
        stories of farm work without the air-conditioned cab,
        stories of simple and hard times.

Grandma's hands
    have changed diapers and disciplined wayward boys,
    comforted scared children and corrected homework,
        guided and nurtured.

Grandma's hands
    have nourished many animals,
        from chickens to cats.

Grandma's hands
    have canned mountains
        of apples, green beans, salsa, jellies, and sauces.

Grandma's hands
    have made more chocolate chip cookies, ice cream, apple pies,
    fudge, dressing with and without onions, and bread
        than can be counted.

Grandma's hands
    have stitched tea towels, calendars, cross stitch, and needlework
        with love and care.

Grandma's hands
         like her
                  have aged

Yet Grandma's hands
         still show the strength
                  of an awesome and beautiful woman.

There is love in Grandma's hands.

Papa

My father,
in white hair whose color matches his mother's,
walks stiffly in order to hide his limp.
A young grandchild beckons
and nothing
not even a searing pain residing in his stump
can impede the progress
towards an inevitable giggle storm
in the form of an impromptu wrestling match.

Later, wire-rimmed glasses askew,
white beard touched with sweat droplets,
face beaming and bright pink,
he is reminded why he grits and bears it.
For this—
a grandchild,
exhausted and sated,
lies beside him
breathing in and out
in and out.

The Talisman

The talisman is not some
great scepter
but a worn flannel shirt so comfortable
to wear it is to put on a second skin
and the two realms of the elders
not great kingdoms
but a simple farm family
and a community of misfits
with whom I have found a home
and a place that unconditionally
claims me
so when I make the presentation
no fanfare precedes me
no company of followers bow
no ceremony ensues
but this does not lessen the honor
with which I make the passing
from elder to elder
one a man with wisdom that awes me
the other a man who shares his story
of surpassing probabilities and seeing God
both men of humility
from whom I will never stop learning
and as I traverse the journey
we call life
regardless of what times may come
these two gentle sages
shall be my polar stars
from whom I guide my ship
through these varying
unpredictable waters.

These little hands

These little hands full of play and dirt
These little fingers covered in paint and glue
So soon will they grow
to labor
and learn
and then
when it's time to fly
these little hands
will wave goodbye

Rocking Lyle, age two, with eyes closed

Oh darling son
for every pair of risings and fallings of your chest
I breathe once

Your soft hair
like that of a duckling's
I caress with a brushing of my lips

These moments
fresh from a nap
or when day's discoveries have wearied you
They land you in my arms
My lap a haven
for how much longer?

Giggles of delight
unhampered by formal civilities
Simple astonishments—
an ant crossing the carpet's threshold
a train's voice traveling the near mile
hiding and re-hiding behind a box
beneath a blanket

I celebrate your innocence
the rolling of your tongue
the lisp of your toddlerhood
ticklish toes and kissable tummy

I am in admiration of your trust

Her Rainbow

For months she hid the secret
curled up in screaming nightmares.
At the home of a paid friend
she was violated in the play house
to the point of questioning her favorite song, Jesus Loves Me.

A Sunday evening,
she says one thing.
A simple sentence, said quietly and meekly.
Her mother catches some of the hidden fear leaking out—
more is going on here.

Later she comes partially open,
not able to release yet the fact
that the policeman's neighbor
directed some of the acts in the front lawn
like an appalling play.

On one of her first outings
after the release of the pain,
something takes her outside early
before Daddy can pay for the groceries.
Mommy! Look up! A rainbow!
Why is it there?
A rainbow is God's promise.
Oh, Sweet Pea. That is your rainbow.
God is promising to keep you safe.

A year later, driving down the road,
her mother says, *Look! A rainbow!*

She replies, *Whose rainbow is that, Mommy?*
Another promise from God.
She is my example of resilience.

How to Live Life… according to my 3 ½-year-old

When you go on a walk to the bank, five blocks,
take an hour to get back home.
Observe each stick,
each crack in the sidewalk,
each different plant.
Delight in the discovery of two snakes
and their stripes and their tongues
and the fact that you can see into their home
through the space between the door and the steps.

Marvel at the yellow beetle stalking a blade of grass.
See beauty in the ants transporting their treasures
after you've moved the stepping stone away.

Be timidly jubilant
at the opportunity to tour an ambulance
because, by chance,
you run into your neighbor cleaning the firehouse.

Ask questions.

Realize that each man and each woman
have the potential to act as daddy and mommy
to someone
and call them that.

Mourn the sunset,
Fight the night because it means a delay in discovery.

Relish cuddles with loved ones.

Enjoy raspberries and being tickled.

Chase cats and dogs just to touch their fur.

See each person's body as a part of God,

      and therefore lovely.

Kiss your mommy at least 8 times each night.

Smile at Daddy when he comes home.

Adore rides in pickups and payloaders.

When reading a picture book, make up your own stories.

Keep your rituals.

It is in the little things that God appears.

Halla, pre-kindergarten, asserts herself

Softest cheek
Bluest eyes
Lush lashes
Mind running faster than your lips
Ears absorbing and retaining more
than is at times fathomable

Grasping at memories
I am paralyzed with awe
not quite knowing how once a sweet babe
has blossomed into you

Assured at times by only yourself
You know what is good
what you desire
and where to lead others

Once fully leaning on my raft
Ever so slowly
It has started—
the drifting apart, anew
so that the lappings of water between
will be connected
not fiercely and firmly, as before
but soon by rope
then a gripping fist
an open palm
a finger tip

I begin to watch you grow
into your own world

Letters to my Son

The next ten poems are a series of letters I wrote during the fifteenth
*   year of my son's life*

Letter One: Cicadas

I am searching for the golf ball
in the grass the same way
I do for movies or books on the shelf—
repeat what I am looking for
again and again in my brain
until what I see matches
what I am thinking—
and on a small appendage
you can barely call a branch
just a foot from the ground
on the nearby pine tree,
there they cling:
five shells…
not dead but once held the living,
newly emerged from the very soil
the pine tree now grasps
even in its state of dying
and their singing in zzz's
you can imitate by pursing
and stretching your lips
surrounds us
and I am reminded how
in the front yard on the ash tree
that bent over our roof
and your dad climbed

with a power saw to trim the branches,
there—
if you looked close enough
and repeated what you were looking for
you would find
their shed exoskeletons fastened
to the bark
until you loosened them
ever so gently
so they could sit among
other little boys' treasures
of rocks and feathers
until dust and time covered them,
swept away one day
and where they settled and clung
now stands a young man
but in the background in the trees
unseen they sing,
their zzz's the soundtrack
to a life lived now a decade and a half
and stretching,
ever growing up.

Letter Two

So I'm thinking of the drawing you did
of an eye
and I realize how it resembles the bloom
of a flower—
the pupil a pistil where the seed later forms,
the iris, where the anthers lie, circles the center,
eyelashes the petals extending outward.
How some flowers like asters
barely have petals at all, like my eyelashes
and some flowers are luxurious
like your sister's.

To bloom
means to grow outward, to expand, to develop
which suggests even a wet stain on a t-shirt
can bloom
or a headache
or a child
and if the eyes are the windows of the soul
and if the eyes are like flowers
then bloom, expand, grow, my child,
for every time I enter a garden
I will be seeking your soul.

Letter Three

I am soil sampling in a corn field
staring down rows
of giant dirty yellow-white spiders,
crown roots and stalks left over
after the farm equipment has been through.
I mention how my boss,
someone 6 inches taller
and at least 100 pounds heavier
didn't have my trouble pushing
the metal probe into the frozen soil
and I realize
you are a good 10 inches taller than me,
almost a whole foot,
the same 10 inches perhaps
you suggest I cut off my long hair
as I did years ago
and donated to Locks of Love
so a child with cancer
can smile in the mirror again;
or maybe so you can draw the clump of strands
before I send it away—
your artistry so professional it looked like my own sketch
you remind me—
as eventually the pupil surpasses
the teacher,
so each generation becomes better than the last
as you will eventually surpass me.
But even now I still

reach out to my parents,
my dad knowing, it seems,
more than anyone in a lifetime could acquire,
admitting I never will quite fill his shoes
just like my own fit completely
inside your sneakers now
before we head out for one of our walks,
me taking two strides for your every one,
but us staying together,
turning together,
walking, talking together,
a way to hold on as this world expands,
as every day you become closer
to being ready to step out further into it.

Letter Four

On days I'm feeling small and cold,
and you are not here,
and there is no one
who will envelop my hands in his
so the circulation will return to white fingers,
I creep into your room, into your closet,
into one of your generous sweatshirts
and hug myself until I feel blood flowing once more.
I now can stand fully under your chin.
You encase me in your arms and we spin
around and around and you say,
Where are you?
as if I have completely disappeared
safely in your embrace.
My wardrobe now includes hand-me-downs
of shirts you have grown out of,
including a brown zip-up hoodie in whose cuffs
you have worried holes.
I press my fingers into them,
and as you are not here,
imagine myself securely enclosed
somewhere
in your mind.

Letter Five

We are waiting for you to finish washing
the dishes,
you proceeding at your own easy pace,
unhurried,
as is your style.
Pressing into your mind some urgency
is exasperating for all
and I am reminded how you and I
are differently wired,
our brains somehow crossing synapses
atypical of those *normies*
whose minds are predictably mapped.
Google would get lost here in our fatty nerve cells.
Your report card is an indicator—
either you get it
or you don't
and to use a word I abhor
it seems your grades are bipolar:
up or down
no middle
only extremes
on or off,
the apple not falling far from its manic–depressive tree.
Don't put us into one of the DSM buckets
for our brains don't quite fit
into one category.
So weekly we pluck, prod, ponder, pensively,
how to best connect you

to this ordinary world,

you who pave your own curiosity,

build your own bridges,

languidly approach each task

arriving into your own

at a time that only belongs to you.

Letter Six

Almost quite literally overnight
here you are a baritone
the weights and conditioning you do at school
assisting in the facilitation of your maturity:
the squaring of shoulders and jaw,
a certain assuredness building,
confidence affecting your stance.
And as if you know the formidability
of your physical stature,
you maintain an attractive amiability
many people have told me they admire.
Not just your humor, your courtesy,
but the hopeful manner in which
you view life—giving the bearer of your attention
the benefit of the doubt.
So when I am frustrated and self-disparaging
I remember that—
after all I have muddled—
when you look at me, observing
the way my barrettes hold back my hair,
you see not horns
but wings.

Letter Seven

You have a certain approach
that lends itself mostly
in the direction of your natural gentle kindness.
Certainly each man falls
along a spectrum of aggression
and your mild nature does not signify
weakness
but rather that the world has not yet given you
sharp edges.
While others are universally coarse and raucous
I hope you contain your own pugnacious testosterone
on the football field.
I know I cannot keep you as you are
but, as you encounter the range of humanity's anger,
learn to be assertive
without becoming scary.
And may you maintain your tendency
towards courtesy and empathy
realizing,
after all,
that these are the makings
of the core
within a real man.

Letter Eight

Because you don't need any more things
and because I'd rather make memories with you
we head off to the zoo for your sixteenth birthday
with your best friend,
you imploring me beforehand
to keep my unusual pun-filled humor
to myself.
But you end up conceding
as even your friend surpasses me in quips.
We search for the metal statue of an elephant,
standing at the end of the bridge
that extends over the koi pond,
its ears outstretched, trunk uplifted,
four feet stolidly planted as if to invite riders.
The same pachyderm that, in 2006, a blond
not-quite-yet three-year-old was lifted onto and,
hanging onto the ears,
grinned while a younger version of me
snapped a photo.
We simulate this, thirteen years later,
you so tall the poor thing seems to have shrunk
over the years,
its head just peeking out from under your legs
with perceptive eyes that say
Here, yes, I remember it well like it was yesterday;
Here time stands still;
Here, you will find magic evermore.

Letter Nine

My parents and I walk toward the bus
after your first game playing football
officially as a sophomore.
The weather is hot, humid, and muggy
and boys eagerly pull off rank and sodden gear
somehow marking their victor's territory
with excessive perspiration.
Being the tallest of the team
you are conspicuous, standing near a tree.
You hug me for such a long time
the sweat and odor permeate my clothes.
Oma giggles,
says, *Wear it like a badge of honor*
and I do
not minding the musky smell
as I drive home peaceably alone,
going from sunglasses to headlights.
I realize proudly that this is a little like life:
there is a holding on and a letting go,
a full sun and a sunset,
each of us in our own orbit;
the sun in a different place in our sky.
Each memory we make is precious,
enabling us to grasp the scent of sunbeams
even after the close of day.

Letter Ten

If I could instill in your mind
only a few pieces of knowledge
I would pull from my grandpa Russ's lips
this saying:
If it's worth doing,
you know it ain't gonna be easy.

And I would emblazon you with the lesson
of F. Scott Fitzgerald's *Adjuster*—
that being grown up means now
you do the work, be the strength,
guide the house, provide the light.

And in everything, when you're at the point
when you want to give up,
give more.
Give a little more than you think you can.
Give a little more than you think you should.
Give more than you feel the other is giving.

If I can't tell you in the right words how to live life,
I will show you resilience, responsibility,
reliability, reassurance, relatability,
and love. Always love.

Poem for a Poet

To my daughter

We stay up to nearly 2 AM
discussing such topics as
aching hips
the best position in which to sleep
trimming hair
which supplements to take when
how to journal
truths about growing out of the first year's
      awkwardness of college
Sociology that overlaps English
      that overlaps Health
      that overlaps Chemistry
as all creation somehow interlinks,
and I find I am connecting now,
grasping moments with a friend
while still guiding a daughter,
we two not only talking of psychologists
      and skin care
but life,
      that which bonds us ever together—
my blood in your veins,
my blue in your eyes,
my nerves in your skin,
my heart beating here
      in every word of this poem for you.

this is just to say...

To Lyle

this is just to say
that one of my cherished memories
is when we played our favorite
country songs to each other,
each taking a turn, and i taught you how
to two-step in the living room
between the couch and the love seat,
one of us jumping to the stereo after
each song, we two getting lost in the hours.

this is just to say
that any seventeen-year-old
might want to relax all weekend
by watching silly shows, but not every
young man wants to hang out doing so
with his mom,
but you did,
and i'm glad.

this is just to say
how proud i am that you are
taking strides in self-reliance,
stepping more and more out
on your own, towards becoming
that grown man i know
i will wake up to find one day
in your place.

this is just to say
that in the selection of a person
to dedicate the playing
of your homecoming football game
i am honored you chose me.

this is just to say
that i know right now money is tight
and things may come hard
and times may be tough
but i appreciate when you paint the deck
and mow the yard
and take out the dead apple tree
with one heavy step of your strong leg
and don't complain
but understand that the more effort
we put into a place
the more it becomes ours.

this is just to say, son
as i look way up at you
and you hug me, envelop me
as only you know how to do
as you warm my hands
in the bitter winters
this is just to say
what words cannot say
sometimes

this is just to say

i love you

Response to my Daughter

We are speaking of the constructs
of gender, and flow from topic
to topic freely and without
shame or constraints, when
I think of the post your
professor wrote describing
a profound statement you
said in reply during a mock
interview. I was suddenly
in awe of your intelligence
and awareness, and relief
at our ability to discuss
openly almost any subject.
I may not brag about you
quite enough, but perhaps
there are not words for
your innate qualities to
find the challenge in each
social situation, to delve
deeper into the complexities
of human nature so well
at such a young age that
leaves me speechless, so
I say nothing, but know
each minute I spend
with you in conversation
is timeless.

Hurry Up I'm Not Ready For This

So I'm driving home
after visiting the graduation parties
of three of my son's friends
when I decide to call my daughter
who is moving her belongings
and cat into my house
from her dorm at the university
and she declares that her father
has dumped it on the lawn
from his trailer and left it all
for her to haul in by herself
and to not freak out but
she has a large quantity
of bags and boxes and whatnots
that will now reside in my basement
until she gets an apartment next year
and perhaps her cat
will stay with me too
when suddenly it gets quiet
because for one thing
I'm thinking
I would never leave my child
with all her things dumped
on the side of the road
all alone to carry them by herself
even if she told me to
and because I'm coming across
the curves in the county road
where you have to slow down
and drive at 45 miles per hour

to not head into the ditch
and because
suddenly
it hits me
my son is graduating
in only a week
and leaving for college
after summer
and my daughter has
one more summer left
before she attends her last year of college
and graduates
to head out
into that big great hungry world
on her own
and I am the parent
of two young adults now
where a small son and tiny daughter
once stood, holding my hands tightly,
me protecting them
from whatever was out there
but now
now it is May
and I have wanted time to stop
and rush by
all at once
I have said
hurry up I'm not ready for this
because now it is here
and my daughter mistakes
my silence for judging
her abundance of material goods

residing in my basement
but how do I tell her
no,
no, it's not that
it's the concept of seeing
both of your footsteps
heading out into the
huge open confusing human race
with no training wheels on anymore,
no longer holding my hand,
with my shield no longer protecting you and
me but a phone call away
but I will still be away and
you will be out in the planet
out there,
taking your first steps alone
and oh, are we ready—
we have all said at some point
haven't we

Hurry up
I'm not ready
for this.

Free

Free, free, set them free
Sting sings
and that's just what you raise them
to do
but sometimes they're more ready
than you are
this slipping from the grasping of hands
to the touching of fingertips
this setting them sail in their own boats,
watching them float away
from your protection.
You open your cupped hands
to release the once injured butterfly
now healed and hatched
grown new brilliant wings
scales iridescent in the sunlight
and the tears in your eyes
smear the sunset and
the clouds floating over the blue.
But this is happy weeping,
the joy of knowing
their journey
is only just
begun.

SUBSOIL

After interacting with the environment, development of soil
structure has obliterated the rock structure of the parent material,
and the soil develops into a subsoil. The subsoil is also called the
B horizon, and is found just above the parent material. It is not as
biologically active or weathered as the topsoil due to the lack of
active water and oxygen circulation. The subsoil contains minerals
and substances that have moved out of the topsoil through leach-
ing by water and gravity. Larger roots will be able to reach this
horizon and utilize the minerals it contains, and it also provides
support for the plants who anchor their roots here.

This horizon has moved away from its parent material, but still
hasn't fulfilled its longing to become an active ecosystem full of
organic activity. The subsoil has some identity issues. It is still
discovering who it is, what that means, and still becoming who it
wants to be.

Tansy Season

Tansy ★ noun ★ [Origin: Middle English-tanesey, Old French-tanesie, Medieval Latin-athanasia, Greek-athanatos—immortal, equivalent to a + thanatos—death] ★ a common weedy composite herb (Tanaceum vulgare) with an aromatic odor, very bitter taste, and finely divided leaves; broadly: a plant of the same genus

sometimes I'll be
standing in a field
and it looks like I'm
doing nothing

I'll tell you
—shhhh—
I'm listening
with my eyes

today I see
a small plant
with lacy leaves
and delicate yellow flowers
in April.
it seems too early
to see blooms
but for these tough winter annuals
this tansy mustard
it's just another day in the sun
and looking small and delicate
is a ruse
for how resilient
Mother Nature
has created her children

that proliferate
this early

a child of the aster family
cousin of the daisy
Tansy's root word is a relative of death
meaning immortality and health

like the bitter yellow tansy
I may be sensitive and small
but am weather worn and
stand through storms
ready for what is blown my way

do not see only with your eyes
but listen closely too
very still
and hear as I do
the small fire within

I am ready for the next season

my tansy season

I am tough
but lacy

delicate
but strong

growing
flowering
ready

every edge cut just so
for you old man weather

this little tansy julie
grows on
blooms on
lives on
tansy—immortal—me

Seeking Home

In a yellow house
In a yellow kitchen
on a farm
in a terraced field
of pollinating corn
far removed
it seems
from everything
I am still swimming
in plastic pools
clutching cats
that cluster and mew at my feet
climbing up the red bud
and under the pine
squinting to reach the sun
on a swing
a yellow swing
and the only thing holding me on
this earth
this soil
save gravity
and the air that takes my breath away
is the ache in
seeking home

I Just Don't Want the Fries Anymore

I'm driving home from my last trip
to the fast-food joint and it hits me:

I don't even want the fries anymore.

I walk into the place and it's right there,
taking up most of the space on the menu:
those value meals with the drink, the sandwich,
and the fries.
It's assumed that's what I came here for;
its assumed that's what people order for meals.

The thing is,
I just don't want the fries anymore.

Sure, I've subbed in onion rings,
but then they overfill me
and I'm left with a stomachache
and a heavy clench in my gut,
stopping me up.

Yup, I just don't want the fries anymore.

Come to think of it,
I wonder if I ever really did.

I ordered them because they were there,
because it's what people around me were doing,
what I thought I was supposed to do.
What if I never liked them in the first place?

Did I ever ask myself if I liked
their greasy, salty, starchy taste?

No, I just don't want the fries anymore.

Sometimes the sandwich alone is all I need.
Sometimes another food satisfies.
So what if it isn't what others are ordering!
This is my body I'm feeding,
so this is my body I'm listening to.

Dude, I don't even want the fries anymore.

Say what you will, try peer pressure,
flash it in pretty lights, tell me I'm unnatural,
tell me it's the norm,
tell me it's against your religion,
I won't listen to what isn't right for me.

I tell you,
I just don't even
          want the fries anymore!

Finding My Exclamation Mark

I always did what I was told
because I never knew what I wanted.
I always became what they said
because I never knew who I was.
I thought I was scared
of the world around me,
ignoring the empty hole marking
the incompleteness within me.
I tried to fill myself with addictions
but nothing filled the ache.
The hole was created from fear
of looking in the mirror,
the wide-open wonder
of what unique light
I could blossom into.
I began the unbordered journey
of merging my disjointed self
with who I could possibly become.

This isn't a path of sure
footedness, but I learned
to hold on with fierce determination;
the pain, eventually, ends.
Step by step, there is no easier
softer way through life
than eyes wide open,
bare skin exposed, showing my self
without a shell. I became
the person I needed to depend on.
Change was the constant

I could count on
until I found my joy.

It takes time to find
the true way to express yourself.
After all, even the typewriter
had to wait almost 100 years
to express excitement;
it took that long for us
to add a button
with an exclamation mark.
Don't waste another day
hiding in fear from the mirror
or from what others might
think. Share your self,
your joy; find your own
exclamation mark and
reveal it to the world!

True Beauty

These stretch marks?
This jiggly jello, bagel belly?
Don't slice and tummy tuck them in.
I've earned every inch.
I've given birth to a baby
the size of a three-month-old child.

This pair of empty worn socks
hanging from my chest?
Don't stuff them
into an ill-fitting push-up
full coverage contraption.
They've fed and nourished,
suckled mouths for months,
providing immunity that no science
could duplicate.

These wobbly wings
on my upper arms?
Don't hide them with long sleeves
in shame during the hot summer months.
They've held toddlers for hours
years after their bodies
were too big to fit
in the carrier car seats
when big eyes and little knees
were too busy for strollers.

These crackled-cracked, sandpaper rough,
scratchy heels and feet

that hold me up?
Don't pumice them away,
hide them in close-toed shoes,
ashamed of the callouses they convey.
These feet have walked miles
in mud and concrete, ice and heat,
past blood and blisters to keep me
on the journey to where I am now.

I will not hide this body
that has travelled more than half
its life already,
just to ease your sensitive eyes
or to conform to what magazines say
is beauty.

I will offer my crooked, timeworn,
veined and soiled hands
for you to hold.
I will walk proudly
on these bowed, muscled legs
with varicose veins that crack in pain
from years of use.

Few will see the allure,
the exquisite grace of a soul
who has lived enough years of anguish and labor
to finally break free
and stand with their scars in the sun.

But I am as nature has made me,
as my history has made me,

as my story has led me,
my map showing here on my skin.

And if you can see the artistry
this world has created in me
open your arms
and touch me.

I will let you in.

Creating Beauty

-1-

Laying scraps of phrases around him,
    the wordsmith plucks at words
        like a gardener gently pulling weeds,
gathering these lost wilting souls in his hand,
    rearranging them in lines
        until they become not weeds,
but a lilting collection of stanzas,
    a poem harmonizing the beauty around him,
        verses declaring the emotions roiling in his soul.

-2-

A composer aligns dots and dashes,
          squiggles and splashes,
                    small round beetles clinging to lines
that musicians grasp—
          a single piano whispers,
                    marching brass blares,
an assembly of strings blossoms,
          wetted reeds play
                    and voices raise into song
so that we relive battles and celebrations,
          moments that left scars on memories
                    and moments we touched God,
peace and heartbreak,
          times of birth and times of letting go,
                    tears and joy.

-3-

Sitting in the audience,
	time and the outside world is erased,
		as each member is drawn into the scenes on the stage,
the playwright having created characters to weep with,
	laugh and sing and spin as they do,
		hearts soaring and breaking when theirs do,
this time a snow globe to be forever suspended
	in a moment until the last word is said,
		the curtain is drawn,
and the spell,
	at last,
		is broken.

-4-

If the world is indeed a stage
        and we the actors upon it
                are we so caught up in the drama
                surrounding us
        that we forget to investigate
what is going on behind the curtain, off stage?

Is our director so perfectly spectacular
        they whisked the curtain around us
                like a magician pulls a tablecloth
        from a fully furnished dining room,
without disturbing even one dish?

Is that curtain the tablecloth dancing
        on a clothesline in the wind,
                mesmerizing us until we are hypnotized
        into disbelieving there is more
than this stage, this play, this scene, this story?

Should we grasp that curtain
        and open the tablecloth into the wind,
                laying open the pulleys and ropes,
        the bodies behind the scenes,
the stars closer to us than ever,

God in our very hands,
        this tablecloth flying to settle
                on a plush green lawn

where we may lay out a bountiful picnic
that feeds every soul,

feeds the minds and the mouths of all,
        fills our hearts with light and breaks the snow globe
                until there is nothing left
        but the great expanse of all the beauty
this universe could ever hold?

It is not too late
      to do something
            beautiful.

Straight-Backed

She took ballet lessons as a child
so has trained herself to always sit
with spine straight, neck poised, chin up,
toes kissing the floor, heels barely
brushing the hard surface, feet ready
to move with the music in her head.
There are no arm rests on the subway,
and the jostling of the man beside her
prevents her grace from flowing shoulder
to fingertips as she grips her bag,
rustling beneath her firm grasp as to
not lose the belongings on to the packed
aisle in front of her. Her elbows clutch
her waistline, trim from controlled eating,
the necessity of skipping lunches
to be able to see each bone of her ribcage,
to float across the dance floor, to float
across life, to control the little she can
in a world that spins beyond her grasp.
Soon she will need to rise
and confront the crowds, become
a part of them instead of standing
on a stage apart, alone and separate,
the dancing phantom on a pedestal
that she becomes when the music begins
and her shoes hug her feet, the curtain
the only cloth that separates reality
from the dream she dances. For now, though,
she closes her eyes from the clashing
chaos around her, pretends to be

empty of emotion, empty of needs,
weightless, hearing only the music
in her head, dancing away
from the world around her.

Ringing the Bell Curve

I had a dream that the pandemic
did not make us afraid to touch
each other, that my previous marriages
did not make me recoil at the attempts
of others to embrace this aged and
weather-beaten body, that children
did not grow up to learn each day
they must attempt to ring the bell curve,
to fit in to the mold we as a society
give them, that I no longer sought solace
or serotonin in a bowl of sugar
or a plate of starch, that the hole inside
each of us was filled with the love
we have for each other, and that is
enough. I woke to the dark cool
of an unfinished night and felt
my kitten curled up between
the pillow and quilt beside me,
kneading her paws on the skin
just below my collarbone. This warmth
of quilt and bodies together,
the heaviness of sleep, the touch of
paw against skin, this was enough,
for now, to fill me. I fell back asleep
to dream of a future where no one
is plotted on a graph of comparisons
and we are not afraid to reach out
to anyone who happens to be near.

Fighting COVID

Sometimes diving into the deep inside us is the only way we rise above it
            —Amanda Gorman, "Essex II"

My fever broke early in the morning
on Thursday
and my bones no longer feel like
they are made of splinters,
piercing me even as I lie still and try to sleep.
My head no longer feels as if
it will soon explode,
though silence still roars in my ears;
my head is still plugged, but
my lungs can breathe again,
though gently.
It is Sunday, I have not seen
a living soul since last Tuesday,
and my mind has taken a journey
to a twisted dark place.
Voices are telling me the world
is forging ahead without me,
and I would not be missed
if I never emerged
from this ever again.
It is as if I am standing
on the edge of a cliff
halfway down into a lonely abyss.
The lack of energy causes
mornings to be lost through sleep,
and my to-do list continues to grow,
as I cannot find the gumption
to complete the items written there.

My brain swims in a fog
and anger surrounds me,
this weekend the last one before
my son moves to college,
a lost opportunity
as he cannot come see me
before he leaves to be
three hours away.
A moment both clarifying
and terrifying
blows a breeze through the fog.
If I jump from this cliff
the fall into the abyss
will most certainly send me
down a destructive path of loss
and regret, if I let the shame
envelop me.
But if I cling to the truth
that this, too, shall pass,
I can imagine this cliff
from the vantage point
of a tall mountain,
and I am standing in front
of a glorious view
that I have stopped to gaze at
during a long journey,
a hike climbing a trail
covered in wildflowers and rare stones,
the view of the snow-covered peaks
and slopes of forested evergreen trees
as I await the breath to return
to my lungs, the ringing to lessen

in my ears, the fog to clear
from my head, the brightness
to return to my eyes.
Because, after all, the difference
between being scared
and being sacred
is merely the twisting
of two letters.
Changing the way I view this cliff
may not immediately lift me
from the dark and twisted place,
but it is a turning point
that lets in a little light,
gives me something to hold onto,
a view to seek as I slowly begin
my climb upwards,
finding each foothold,
each place my hands can grasp
to pull me out of here.

Off There

I look up
with my
round blue white eyes
wide and pressed
into my eyelids

The snow
catches my eye lashes
      and they dance with the breeze back and forth back and
forth but still suspended on my lashes I feel them tickling me so
soft and cold they are like men moaning and groaning clinging to
their jail bars yet they don't know they're truly happy or maybe
they're like hors d'oeuvres stuck on a
                      toothpick

And as I
look up
I see
the pink and green
watercolors
      smeared
         together
domed
        above
        me

Shopping for Poems

Fresh out of ideas and inspiration,
I go shopping for poems.

Among the words and phrases,
similes mix with metaphors;

semi-colons get tangled with quotation marks
and rhyming words walk hand in hand.

Twisting trees turn torridly
toward the torment of drought

while crouching clouds clench lightning bolts
before throwing them at dancing tornadoes and bouncing hail.

Cracked soil sits beside ponded puddles,
and mermaids sip pearled green tea

while sighing of romances held
between their fingertips.

I'm flooded with hummingbirds
darting in a swarm of bees,

looking for untouched prairies
singing of unmown grass

and open-eyed flowers with sweet-scented nectar
flowing from their centers.

Nightmares shy into the abyss
when the sun comes out,

but at night,
I hear they roam the shadows

and skip in the spaces between the spiderwebs
at the notice of a mere slight breeze.

I reach in for these poetical delights,
but every time I plunge my hands in

I bring them back up empty,
everything running through my fingers like water;
a sieve.

What is Wrong with my Poems?

You write them raw and untethered,
as if you close your eyes
and look the other way
while your hand scratches them out,
these feral poems that reveal
the animal side of our human existence
no one wants to admit is a part of us.

You don't coddle them,
don't cup them in your hands
and form them lovingly out of clay,
don't dress them up in pretty lace
and fancy gowns but
let them run naked and screaming
through the streets in tatters
just as they are,
without make-up or paint or corsets.

You allow beauty to waltz
with the grotesque hand in hand,
when all we want to see in ourselves
is the formed miracle spiraling upward;
we don't realize you offer us a gaze
at ourselves in the mirror
with each swipe of your graphite
covered fingers.

Dizzy

S
W
I
 R
L
I
N
G
as a little toy
T
O
 P
--
F
A
L
 L
I
N
G
I crash at the bottom
        of my little
water
        WOR
LD.

Freefall

lying on back on bed
tears leave eyes
tears cross cheeks into ears
toothless cat licks them away
it's okay
mind is thinking again
mind is broken
broken brain
brainbreak not heartbreak
heartbreak?
hearts can't break
made of muscle
muscle is meat
muscle rips
heart of gold
heart of iron
iron bends
heart of steel
heart of glass
hairline fracture
clean break
open crack
leaking out
ewww what is that?
trying to hide
instead of hide,
bare it all?
bare it all
open up
open wide

closet door open
light is on
see all the cracks
clean the cracks
pick on the cracks
pick bones clean
clean and empty
empty hole
holes in stories
pick at the holes
worm holes
birds' claws pick at worms
bury it all
bury the laughter
bury in dirt
the dirt I could dig up on you
hide your face
hide from view
hide in crowds
hang head
slump shoulders
swing arms side to side
walk in crowd
part of the masses
one of the many
look like them
oh don't you know
how different I really am
from you
Am I you?

You Are

You are remembering the poet from
this weekend, the moment you walked
up to her to introduce yourself,
the second time you have heard her
read from her most recent book,
how your mind went blank, all words
dropped from your vocabulary,
like the time you were supposed to
give out your boss's phone number
to a client but you forgot the numbers
five and six, forgot them entirely,
like the moments in the movies where
a person in love approaches their crush
and is unable to utter a single word,
and you are baffled by the human brain
and still a bit embarrassed, wondering
if you should contact her and apologize
somehow or if that would make it worse,
wondering why it is you can write hundreds
of poems and years of blogs but stutter
when it comes to the spoken word, wondering
if this means you somehow have a crush on her
and didn't realize it, but isn't she so much
younger than you and you don't know
anything about her, thinking now of
all of the things you could have said to her,
how even the start of the poem could have
led in so many directions it left you
drowning in words, you are my sunshine,
you are not alone, you are important,

you are the reason I get up in the morning,
you are all that and a bag of chips,
you are the cream in my coffee,
you are so right, you are funny,
you are wonderful, you are crazy for thinking
all this and isn't the mind such a confusing
but surprising part of us, keeping us spinning,
spiraling thinking wondering until we are
exhausted forced to rest and recover,
eventually accept this is just the way
you are.

Forced Passage, Breathing Dust

This here, is a new passage
to a new time
for which the destination
is not fully revealed.
Though you may have been forced
to travel the path
look to the valley
while breathing in this dried humus,
this dust flying
swirling through your hair,
in your nostrils, between your fingers.
You are not the only one on this journey
though it is yours solely to tread,
your burden, your story,
your purpose only to fulfill,
to open and expose to the very particles
you now breathe.
Dance to any melody
trudge tiny moments
rest only upon reaching the grassy plain
where legs may stretch
sun surely shines
and passages reveal
dust turned to glitter.

Cowboy Trail, early evening

On your left
passing you twenty-somethings
on this trail.
I may be short
but my legs are long and strong.
My life may have surpassed four decades
but my heart. beats. still.
Breaths come in full and deep and even.
Goose and frog
Pup and songbird
express jubilance among my pheromones.
The sun and I
old friends
race each other
headed
in opposite directions.

Cherry Tomatoes

I need to wash my cherry tomatoes
freshly picked from the garden,
the small red globes no bigger
than the tips of my fingers,
but first I must grasp each one
and remove the green cluster
of sepals attached to the stem,
these dried leftover flower parts
looking like small spiders
scattered and skittering
in the bottom of the bowl
as I tilt it
to empty into the trash can,
and place the colander
of red round balls
under the spray of water
to rinse the dirt that clings to their skins
until I can reach into that pile
of jacketed juice spheres,
gather a few, dripping,
into my mouth, and bite down,
their taste bursting forth
against my cheeks and tongue.

Of Life

Inspired by Walt Whitman
I will sing of the ordinary
the every day
I will sing

I will sing of walls painted faded canary yellow
peeking through two coats of primer and morning glory blue
staring at me, still peeking yellow

I will sing of life
of that entity science has not named
in its search for what makes us tick
not only of life created through sperm and egg
through Deoxyribonucleic acid and cells
dividing and drinking

but the wonder of my cat's multicolored whisker
her raccoon tail and key lime eyes
cream mixed with smoke
salmon foot pads and nose, nudging
Jolie kneads my lap, finding it comfortable in the sun

while her sister, Wunder, keeps watch over our daughter
shedding midnight black fur starting to grey in tiny patches like stars
softest I've ever touched
squeaking her half meows
watching me cross the room with her moon eyes
How do molecules make her who she is?

I will sing of the survivor's scar
stretching across skin above muscle and bone

dotted with memories of stitches
Tracing the depression of its path
I wonder how a scar can feel by not feeling
nerves absent from scar tissue
etched in such smooth skin
skin that once was split, once parted, now fused whole
and healing

I will sing of skin the colors of the earth
of ivory, pale rose, charcoal,
of hazelnut, coffee, chestnut,
of roasted red pumpkin, apricot, butternut squash
I will sing of beauty in the diverse
we from the soil are the very colors of
the soil but many horizons within, blending

I will sing of the plains
with rolling hills and dancing prairie grass
laughing water trickling over rocks and sand and soil
dust whipped by the wind
I will sing of the plain
the ordinary

I will sing

Seeking the Spectacular

Day 1

I go to the mountains
        to seek the spectacular.
My son reminds me
        as my daughter drives the car west
and they seem to grow as we approach
        that the mountains stay the same size,
        that I stay the same size;
it is only the distance between us
        that is changing.
A physical distance between three cars
        and seven bodies closes
        as the day's hours bend
        into late afternoon.
An emotional distance closes
        between one family
        as the week marches slowly
        day by day
        in a cabin
        in the mountains
seeking the spectacular.

Day 2

We wake each morning
with the mountains standing
beside the sunrise,
shadows creeping up the slopes
as the hours pass
and we sip coffee
out of borrowed cups
in quiet wonder
before discussing our plans
for the day's excursions.

Day 3

Assembling in repose
on the porch of the cabin
as we rename the snow-topped
squared-off peak in the distance
after my son, who yearns to
hike up to its summit,
the wind blows intermittently
through the trees,
as if it is the mountains
around us breathing.
The same wind makes
my mother stop mid-hike
in the forest
and smile.
She pauses to listen
to the pine and aspen trees
speaking low,
whispering to each other
under their breaths.

Day 4

We are enamored
by the ambivalence of the wildlife
surrounding us.
Tawny beige deer with large cone ears
graze near cars and cabins,
looking up at passers-by
with wide dark eyes.
Elk with umber coats and
ecru tail ends hide near ponds
and under trees,
lying in patches of grass
just out of reach.
Swallows dip and glide
for unseen insects,
returning to nests under eaves
and in nearby trees.
A falcon lands and races
after a family of prairie dogs,
their short fluffy tails wagging
as they rush to hide in their holes.
Black, grey, and flashing
metallic green hummingbirds
flit by with sounds
of thrumming,
of an electrified bumblebee,
whizzing by so quickly
each tiny winged being
can scarcely be seen

by the naked eye
except when they pause
at a bent knee, a red sweatshirt,
a sweet can of cola, or
a resting walking stick.
A pika and chipmunk peek out
from a cluster of rocks
on the side of a mountain.
A ground squirrel
uses sign language to implore us,
passing hikers, to feed its tiny paws
and upturned mouth
with forbidden snacks
that we keep stashed in our packs.
Each feathered and furred creature here
is a part of this world
and we humans
are merely visiting.

Day 5

My son, my twin, and I
go hiking in the Rockies.
We trek around Lily Lake,
climbing rock stairs
where we almost lose the trail
and stand on outcroppings
to look at the small road
and clear water below.
We slide on mud and snow
to Calypso Cascades
where the waterfall greets us
with a cold chill and
crashing splash across
a series of multicolored
boulders.
We zigzag up Deer Mountain
into a world of jutted rocks
and twisted rooted trees,
a magic place we imagine
fairies hold tea parties,
dwarves meet on stacked boulders,
and trolls sit for picnic lunches
among the narrowing path.
Small white flowers
surprise us by popping out
in the middle of a trail,
bushes and trees find homes
growing between rocks in

impossible places,
branches bend against the years
of wind beating at them,
creating old men and arms
where trees should stand.
In this magic place,
snow flurries sparkle
against our faces, but disappear
before ever alighting
on the ground.
Each step here
is a passage into another
dimension, another time,
another land altogether.

Day 6

I would move mountains
        mountains moving
                mountains haven't always

been here, mountains grew
        from tectonic plates shifting,
                mountains giving way

mountains now giving by standing
        mountains giving us a place
                to escape, giving peace,

giving splendor, giving spectacular
        views, mountains made of rock,
                rocks that aren't forever

either, rocks that erode into minerals,
        minerals that mix with
                the organic, the carbon

and minerals together that
        create the soil, the soil
                that covers the earth,

the earth that grows the plants,
        the plants that feed
                the animals, the animals

of which we are a part, so we are
    all living, all changing,
        even the rocks

the mountains, even in their way
    are breaking and breathing,
        in their way are living,

the mountains in their way
    are giving to earth, and
        we are all here

not worthy of growing on this
    round cycling planet of earth
        we call home.

Day 7

So in my week in the mountains
surrounded by family and nature
have I found the spectacular?

Have I found the spectacular
in a snow-capped peak
fourteen thousand feet high?

Or in an electric-sounding
black and metallic green
tiny hummingbird,
skirting the sagebrush?

Have I found it in the
twisting of the branches
and roots of the pine tree?

Or the singing of the wind
through the aspen leaves?

Have I found the spectacular
in fifty years of marriage
between my parents,

two souls who found each other
and hung on, despite
the difficulties?

Have I found the spectacular
in the footsteps of my sister,
the arms of my son's hug,
the conversations with my daughter?

Have I found the spectacular
climbing a two-story wall
for the first time,

or hitting a bullseye
in archery?

Can the spectacular be found
in the symbiotic relationship
of lichen clinging to a rock
on the side of a mountain?

In a gathering of three generations
sitting around a fire
in a borrowed cabin in the woods?

Or in a tiny snowman,
gradually melting in the sunrise
on the last day of a vacation

as the shadow creeps up the slope
at a high altitude
on the second to last day of May?

Perhaps, even
the spectacular can follow me home
to my garden

where my seeds are starting
to push through the soil,
new life here on this earth,

so varied
so vast

so breathtakingly
spectacular.

Goodbye

Goodbye to artificial authenticities
and shimmering illusions
dancing over the rippling water
that will take you under
into the grey beyond speckled
with cottoned regrets of yesteryear
as you grasp what could have been—
only faded lights streaming in
that you can no longer hold on to.
No my dear, rise up
past turbid torments and
tortuous tornados of guilt,
beyond the abysmal arbor
where fears reach out to grab you.
Goodbye to all that would keep you back
and hold you down into this
voracious valley of darkness and defeat.
Go on. Fly on. Run on. However
you proceed, do it with grace
and resilience and grit, resting only
to enjoy the views and renew strength
to continue on your journey towards
peaceful pastures and tranquil trees
where waters run clear and
your mind does not spin. Yes, dear,
press on, the light is true, and
you will make it step by step.

TOPSOIL

Above the subsoil is the horizon with the most advanced structure, having interacted with the ecosystem the longest. The topsoil, also called the A horizon, has access to a whole host of exchanges to help its development. Containing the soil organisms (think earthworms, millipedes, mites, insects, and larvae), fungi (a kingdom more closely related to animals than plants), soil microorganisms, plant roots, minerals, and nutrients, it is the most biologically active horizon. The A horizons are the areas of the most organic matter accumulation due to this activity, their decomposition, and resulting stabilization. If the topsoil has been disturbed by humans, it is an Ap horizon, or called a plow layer.

You could say this is the horizon that clings the closest to nature.

Morning

The coolest time of day
full of dew and promise
Hours open before you
The sun yet rising
Flowers facing the beams
following the warmth across the sky
as the day lengthens
Did you know
if the sun is not available
to retain warmth
sunflowers will face each other?
On those mornings
when you awake
and clouds obscure your skies
threatening storms
On those bad days
my dear
instead of lamenting the grey
Look not to the lightning
nor drown your sorrow in the rain
but turn your face instead
towards mine
and we shall be
each other's light

Tasting Plants

False Spring has me standing
at the foot of my garden,
soil bare and blowing
into my nostrils, the dry dirt
a dusty crunch that lands
onto my tongue as I open my mouth
on this windy day.
I can taste the minerals in the soil
as they await roots to find them,
the tiny plantlets growing inside
in assorted pots along my windowsill
until the temperature warms
and I can transport them outside
where their roots can expand and grow
and deepen, and instead of
restrictive manufactured soil
in a plastic boundary, the plants
will stretch out and have
free reign over every expanse
of my square of garden,
able to find the sun and earth.
And I wonder as these green shoots
reach for the sky
and their roots drink in
the water and nutrients,
do they taste each drop
of crystallized sky in the water,
and the tangy salt
of the minerals as each ion
crosses their membranes?

As their root hairs reach out,
do they develop a
preference for nitrogen,
does phosphorus leave
a sour aftertaste,
is magnesium a little metallic
in its saltiness?
Is it more refreshing
to absorb water right after a rain,
or does sipping on morning dew
equate to our wake-up
with a cup of coffee?
How delightful is the feeling
of the organic matter I place
before watering,
especially right after a dry spell
that has started to create cracks
in the soil of my yard?
How glorious to look up
and taste the sweet sugar
you have created
from the warmth of the sun
shining down.

Waking the Zombie

I flick on the porch light
and for once I am glad to have
attracted two white flapping moths,
their bodies settling on my screen door,
close to the glow that brings them forth.
I am relieved to see that they have
brought with them a couple of
dark grey gnats, tiny flying dots, for company.
I am sighing because this means
an end to the cold winter months
when I frigidly stay indoors, wrapped
in layers of so many clothes and blankets
I forget what my own body looks like,
evenings of frozen exhaustion
from the disappearing sun,
caged like an animal in the dark.
I am smiling because this means
an end to feeling like the walking dead,
my unused muscles and white purpled skin
hanging off me like a zombie
in my son's apocalypse movies,
walking stiff legged, working out kinks
and groaning, seeking nourishment,
and nothing but the green of buds
and that warm humid air,
my tulips peeking out,
birds quarreling over prime real estate,
those small signs that spring is
around the corner, nay, spring is here!,
even the gnats and moths beating,

clinging to my light,
will exhume this dead heart
and revive my spirit,
teach me to live again.

Tones of Seedtime

The county map
spread on the desk at work
is sprinkled with polka-dots,
indicating each place with a permit
to burn their unwanted.
My son has started wearing
his form-fitting swim shirt
and my daughter has unearthed her shorts.
I've raked the dead plant residue
to view green emerging from soil.
My husband talks of mowing the lawn soon
and has pushed our snow blower deep into the garage.
Cats have more hours to sprawl in the sunlight
and perch on windows to fling
their broken arpeggio cries
to birds frolicking in the yard.
We each display our own
symptoms of spring.

May Springtime

Like magic, slowly,
tiny green heads are pressing their way
out of the deep soil
where months ago
ag bags would lie lifeless,
looking like great white snakes,
their bodies full of Mother Stalk's gift
of kernels, given the previous autumn,
waiting all winter on the dull
bare ground,
as if these behemoth beasts
could rise up blunderingly,
slither off slowly,
and envelop or absorb their neighbors,
awaiting in the mixture of
gold, grey, black, and brown
blended background,
now gone
into their holes
and new life
though small
but promising
is bravely presenting hope
to the landscape.

Driving from Bellevue, NE to Oklahoma City, OK

A crimson pasture is rimmed with
lime and hunter green trees,
here and there surprised by a redbud.

The soil is wet and covered
with pooled water where it has been planted.

A white and brown speckled hawk
startles into the air as we pass,
flying between the rain drops.

Cattle look at us with indifference.

The first sign of the south
are oil rigs
dipping up and down,
looking like some strange mantis.

Droplets push up on the windshield
after a light rain.

Dirty grey cotton balls move above
and hold us in a wet soggy fog.

Rain high in creeks reminds us
that things happen when we're here
things happen when we're not here
and things will continue to happen
whether we're here or not.

Racing the Storm Home

I'm distractedly putting together
a shipment of sorghum for some folks
in western Nebraska and Kansas
and blocking out racing worries
about missing homework and lackadaisical actions
causing my son to just barely
graduate high school in a couple of days
when in walks my supervisor
with a concerned and hurried look on her face
and I think *what have I done now*
but she is telling me
to pack up my computer and get home
because a bad thunderstorm is coming fast
and I should leave now
to make it back to town in time
before it hits
so I'm driving down the highway,
my little car beaten by gusts of wind
blowing the storm in behind me,
staying physically ahead of
the clouds rushing the rain in,
but unable to outrun the
spinning subconscious recitations
revolving in my brain,
these squeals becoming more persistent
as the storm quickens
and the wind blows harder,
as if the thunder is carrying them along
in a rucksack slung across
its wide loud shoulders.

But I pull into my drive
and hasten into my house
just as the sky turns green
and the clouds let loose
an abundance of water soaking
not only the fertilizer into
my hungry rooting yard,
but every inch of every thing
still out in the open
under the sky out there.
And I look on,
thoughts still spilling
out of the storm's forgotten backpack,
shrugged off once the lightning struck
and ran off with the thunder,
laughing.

Soybean Gall Midge

An insect so tiny,
the striped fly-like adult
is rarely found, and orange larvae
can only be seen by the
naked eye once it has
already gouged out its place
in the stem of a soybean plant,
how do you conquer an entire
living thing on your own?
You obliterate the plant,
your damage disguised
as another disease, so we humans
didn't even know you existed
until years after you had
ravaged our fields.
For such a minute being, you
had the gall
to beat us at our own game
and now we are scrambling
to fight you,
oh midge that sneaks in
from copses of trees and
grassy strips, then silently
and fleetingly slips out
again, leaving wilted leaves
and promises for new generations
in your wake.
Our production is humbled
and our research is baffled
by your proliferation.

Mother Nature continues
to surprise us
with her creations.

Dying Mantis

Dying for longer than 24 hours,
I gave her a rose to watch as she did.
The boy who stepped on her
was unaware of the green beauty
he left behind.
Still combative the next day
in the cup I set her:
Oh please dear mantis
say a prayer for me.

Playing with Grasshoppers

On my weekly sojourn to the fields
I find myself
playing with grasshoppers.
In the unmown ditch I must
wade through
we play hide and seek
as I chase them on my way into the field.
A yellow juvenile sitting in the collar
of a corn leaf
moves each leg as I touch it, unknowingly
engaging in pattycake with me.
Walking down a row, a corn plant leans
so low that the tassel greets me at
eye level and, clinging to it,
a full-grown grasshopper
moves side to side with me
as if to say, *Peek-a-boo.*
In the mundane of our day-to-day tasks
we must find a way
to stay young.

Beeline Redefined

If a bumblebee will take a detour
from the task of feeding on flowers
to playfully roll and pull on toys,
doing somersaults,
and if honeybees can count
and change their behavior
based on the difficulty of the task,
then perhaps we are in a world
where this earth contains
many more sentient creatures
who can feel, emote, sense,
and express feelings
than we humans were once aware.
We knew dogs play fetch just
for fun, and a cat will curl up
and prefer an owner's lap,
showing love, but science's discoveries
of orcas playing in shallow waters,
apes showing empathy, and
dolphins creating language
reveals a bigger picture
of the interconnectedness
of our role on this planet
and the possibility that
a spirit truly resides
in every living thing here.
And if there is an awareness
in every being that changes
we are propelled to the further urgency
that we respect each connection

our life intersects, to respect
the importance of honoring playfulness
in the perpetuity of our planet.

Popcorn Frogs

This summer,
engaging in a favorite hobby,
that of catching critters of any crawly kind,
we process slowly
around the pond.
A smattering of tiny froglets
at the edge of the water
bursts into all directions
in reaction to cupped eight-year-old hands
smacking the mud.
With delight, my son responds
they're like popcorn!
How lucky to have found this small space
in time
on earth
to let the tiny things
hold significance.

Intelligence isn't Reserved for Humans

The word intelligence implies one is wiser
when their knowledge is shared; the word
tell is imbedded within its letters.

But sometimes it is better to live the
solitary life, as we octopods have discovered,
being secretive and retiring along the ocean floor.

We may be complete with only a head and arms,
but we aren't all soft-bodied; we have a sharp beak
that can quip clips in return,
helpful when eating our shellfish.

Our wardrobe appears simple and universal—
every one of us wears a skirt—but we can change
the texture and color of our skin so rapidly,
with only a fleeting thought.

Since we have no backbones,
you humans have passed us over for years,
thinking us simple creatures appropriate for
your plates and zoos and aquariums.

But we are attentive to our eggs until they hatch
as tiny replicas of us,
a mere one-third of a centimeter long.

We use stones and your discarded trash
as doors to our dens, carry coconut shells as houses,
dutifully solve the puzzles and toys you hand us
in captivity.

We are not a creature that likes to feel jailed,
although you fondly call us mischievous, sneaky,
and ingenious; we are trying to gain our freedom
from your cages and can recognize your faces
as you look in on us from the other side of the glass.

For fun, we play with our food—
we tap it on the shoulder; when it jumps in surprise
away from us, we catch it with another waiting arm
and into our hungry mouths.

Don't fool with us.

We have nine brains to your one,
three hearts to your single, broken beating muscle;
our blood beats blue and true
and we will someday swim and crawl
right over all of you.

Fungi

As old as time
Mother mycelium
stretching nerve-like
in every grain of soil,
a weblike brain
capturing carbon,
an alternate consciousness
recycling and transforming,
recreating,
the end and the beginning,
neither animal nor plant
but connecting both worlds
in electric currents,
synapses firing beyond miles
of each hypha, each spore,
each cell promising
a responsive continuation
of life on this earth,
a certainty of eternity
in every corner of this
our amazing and ever changing
earth.

Owl

You nocturnal bird of prey
waiting on telephone poles and in trees
as we walk at night
to swoop down for your supper
or blink sleepy-eyed on my doorstep
as we disturb your slumber
cleaning gutters on our house.
I sat beside a small screech
caged at the park once
being protected as he healed from
a broken wing.
He winked at me, the small broad head
dominated by two golden moons for eyes
directed forward
with tufts for ears worn regally
and a bit ragged
as he waited for a chance to see the sky
and glowing orb of night once again,
wanting to hunt freely without bars
or enclosures,
seeking the time to spread his wings,
newly mended.

Eagle, Hawk, Killdeer, Chickadee

Some people say it is luck
to see a bald eagle or hawk
so you would think I'd be more fortuitous
seeing hawks and eagles nearly every
trip to the field.
Yesterday, it was a bald eagle
perched high in the tallest tree,
then two hawks circling,
hunting together.
A set of killdeers called out
from the sandy wetland
and a pair of chickadees
who nest near my office
greet me each morning as I walk by.
Perhaps Mother Earth's way of blessing
is from an alternate vantage point.
My luck isn't the number of times I've failed
or the ways I prove inadequate.
My favor is in the ability to withstand loss
and the family who accepts my brokenness.
It is in the soaring eagle I see
and the fawn I come across unexpectedly.
It is in each green thing I watch
push through the soil each spring.
It is hope, and resilience, and life.

Keeper of the Plants

With thanks to Pat Meiergerd's fields

Crying circling hawk
flitting meadowlark
twittering red-wing blackbird
all know me.
They sing to me.
I am the Tansy Julie,
keeper of the plants.
The birds know this
as I fly in my own way
down rows watching my green ones
emerge from the soil.
The birds they sing to me
Fly, soar, our Tansy Julie,
you fingered eagle with broken
mended wing, guide these rooting babies
to stretch their leaves to the sky.
Soar, Tansy Julie,
sing to us with your thoughts, your eyes,
honor us with your pen,
find some harmony here to heal
and we will not ruffle feathers,
finding peace under the big blue dome
covering us all.

Meadowlarks

I saw a family of meadowlarks today
congregating in the grass in front of me.
They didn't stay long enough for a photo,
flitting to the evergreens nearby
when I came towards them.
The atmosphere was joyful,
that of a party I disturbed.
The trio was not perturbed,
merely moved the festivities upward,
dancing among the branches
and singing,
their yellow plumage paying homage
to the sun
and summer.
I left them to their happy chirps,
going on my way
a bit more chipper myself.

The Supervisor's False Predator

We were attempting to put in stepping stones
and it was taking twice the effort than we thought it would.

This robin would come within arm's reach
of us, feathers ruffled in a distinctive wind-swept style.

He would wait for us to upend the soil
and then his lunch would swim to the surface
in the wheelbarrow where he perched, tilting his head.

We called him our supervisor; we were the axis
about which his world was turning, for the moment,
until, exhausted, we put the brakes on the whole project.

I encountered this same robin the next weekend
when I brought out my domesticated cat, a false predator,
to sit on the patio with me after doing yard work.

The robin with ruffled feathers went straight to alarm mode
although my cat paid no interest in the bird,
lying down on the edge of the pavement as I sipped my coffee.

Ever the supervisor, the robin took earnest in his plight,
perched on a metal post, in the midst of a verbal anxiety attack.

What I didn't see until later was his flightless youngling
sitting on the ground below, a child for which this parent volunteered
    to bleed.

False Rain

The cloudless sky's blue face stares at me
each morning as I cross the yard,

my footsteps making the dry grass
crunch beneath my weight when
I miss the stepping stones, and

I drive off to work for what seems like
another endless weekday without rain.

When I return, the soil is so dry
it has shrunk into jagged puzzle pieces
across the crackly brown lawn
where green should be growing.

Though I will literally pay for it later,
I drag the sprinkler and hose out

and set it where the ground looks
unforgivingly beyond repair,

and walk to turn the spigot on,
which squeaks in protest.

Suddenly there is artificial rain
in my yard, and the cool droplets
that spray my face and arms
surprise me as I walk beneath its reach.

Birds gather at the margins
of this shower, waiting for worms

to surface for breath as the water
fills the cracks.

We have all been waiting
for grey skies far too long already.

This small drink will barely
slake the thirst of these dying
rooted beings, and until

the clouds roll in,
the skies open up
and the soil truly breathes again,

they shall sleep,
broken and brown,

hoping to hold on.

Sorry for the Rainy Season

The drought has persisted
as if God has been saying,
Sorry for the rainy season,
sorry for the ruined leather jacket
you wore in the thunderstorm,
the soppy seats in the car when
you left the windows open overnight.

Wind blows chickadees flying
and they tumble like leaves
falling off trees,
dry dancing balls of fluff
unable to fly, dust coated wings
grabbing air currents too strong
to carry song.

But there is promise of rain tonight.

The last of this day is passing
like a cat bounding toward
a food bowl, full, newly placed
on the floor. Racing head first,
furry paws slipping, spread eagle
on a polished laminate surface,
no way to stop gracefully
before the finish line.

I look up to see grey storm clouds
like mammoths, crying above us
at the cracks in the soil
big enough to stick your hand in.

Simply the Best

I look forward to experience
simply the best sensation
in late summer after warm air
and long hours of daylight
have caused my indoor potted plants
to flourish so well their roots are bursting
past the capabilities of their current pots
and I proceed to find them new homes
in which to grow.
Simply the best sensation
as I take each plant and remove it
from its former living space
is that slightly fungal
moist earthy smell
of newly wetted soil
falling between my fingers and under my fingernails
spilling into the new vessels,
slightly larger dwellings
for my growing plants.
Quite happy in their sun-dappled windows,
light streaming through,
protected from weather,
breathing for and with me,
we here
are growing together.
Nothing better
than the feeling of soil between my fingers
and something solid to hold on to.

Entering Autumn

The leaves on the trees bunch together
leaving geometrical shapes the color of the sky
in between.
It is early September.
My son has turned six.
We have honored nine eleven with a moment of silence
on radio
only two days ago.
Across the street at a neighbor's house,
my son walks away from a friend,
his index finger extended, pointing up—
our universal sign for *just a minute.*
Somehow knowing the days are growing shorter
he must fit it all in before winter.
He walks toward his bike,
dons a helmet,
and proceeds to race time
as the sky slowly dims above him.

The Personality of Trees

In autumn I observe the personality of trees.
The Ash is hurried, turning bright yellow and dropping early
before the others can think to join him.
The Pin Oak is pensive and shy,
sometimes just going from green to brown,
only once in a while including a deep orange-red fire
before reluctantly letting go near the end of the season.
The Maple is outgoing, exotic, and bold,
changing her colors to bright orange and red,
showy and gradually dropping her leaves throughout the season.
The Linden leaves die laboriously and dramatically,
providing us with a brilliant yellow.

New Job

It used to be the road would take me
past rolling straight rows of green turned gold,
through passages of pollen and grain.
I would watch soil bring forth new life
where before was only a line of buried kernels.
What is poetic about computers and accounting,
shipping and invoicing,
taking the sale from sold seed
to your front door?
Today autumn was truly upon us,
the chill in the air as tangible
as the tips of my fingers.
Walking towards the office I saw
sitting on the packed gravel,
too cold to move,
blood slowing thick like antifreeze,
a sphynx moth,
its large striped body still, waiting
for the sun's warmth to allow movement of wings
to carry it upward.
I greeted the creature,
cupped it carefully in my hands,
and, laying the moth safely under a nearby tree,
thanked God that today
I had been useful
to someone, somehow.

Sparrows and Finches

In the warm afternoon autumn sun
golden gleaming through my window
I hear a quiet tap tapping.
I turn to see a small house sparrow
and her party of friends alight
on the bush outside,
picking at the twigs and the last
of the leaves clinging to the small branches
yet, a deep brownish magenta shaking
from their urgent picking.
Once in a while, one of the small creatures
sits on the bottom ledge of my window, then
POPs!
her little head up and looks in
for a few seconds, then
flies quickly away.
It is as if she is asking me
to remember the days I felt
the heartbeat of Mother Nature beating
deep within her soil, beneath the grassy skin
of her, the days I felt the breath
of her wind blow across my cheeks
and in my hair, to remind me
her pulse still courses through
rivers and streams and
if I listen hard
on those days I walk on the trail
among the trees
she calls to me still,
Mother Nature's voice the song

the leaves make as they shake,
the grass makes as it bends,
the river as it races over rocks
and against its banks.
And on those days I'm feeling lost
and out of place, I can listen once again
to align my heartbeat with hers,
breathe softly with the wind,
feel the pulse of the earth all around me
and know that this, here, is where
I belong.

Moving Diana

It is time
for raking leaves, trimming dead foliage
and moving the rocks
to anticipate new landscaping.
The boys tote piles of stones via wagon
while my daughter finds them hidden in the dead weeds
on an atypically warm day in November.
Time has already changed
so darkness hastens its gradual tendons
all too soon.
One ornament that must be carried carefully
whose origin has a tale of its own
is my headless fountain statue.
I call her Diana
and she moves about the front yard;
once near my roses,
once at the foot of the stairs,
once propped by the railing to ascend.
Now Diana sits
white and pensive
almost leaning beneath the ash.
She is waiting;
patiently waiting and asking,
When is winter?

It is early

November and fields of corn
have not been harvested yet
Armies of resilient warriors stand
crowded in rows
Some broken at the waist
Stalks clenched
Gone from green to golden to brown towards grey
Brittle not hollow yet
Roots grasping saturated ground
Waiting for the wind to finish blowing the soil dry
Wombs of kernels drooping but holding on
Each a papoose with so many teeth
until beasts driven by computers
once hunkered down, breathe to life again
lights flashing
come to sever and cut each soldier
Tear open the ears to swallow the grain
belching out stover in tatters behind
So this winter each airplane and satellite
hell bent on going anywhere but here
will look down
and see nothing but brown

Wind Storm

What we have here
is a failure to
calm Mother Nature
from a cold-shouldered temper tantrum,
the unending tirade bursting
from a mouth that needs
to be closed,
pushing cars on the highway
like an upset toddler
rocking a doll roughly held
from the tips of its
clumped hair,
this love affair between
the low- and high-pressure systems
having gone on way too long,
an abundance of evidence
that opposites do not meld
in a cohesive manner,
the stinging sleet and slamming
of my door before I am completely inside
proof enough we must
split these two apart
before the mother completely
loses her cool and causes more damage
than any of us can mend.
The only question is,
will I be able to find my trash can
once I get home from work tonight?

Grateful Sunshine

Stepping briskly, one foot in front
of the other, down my regular route
in the neighborhood where I now live,
I race the downing of the sun;
I have been craving this day
of milder weather,
waiting out the frigid cycle
of immobility and loss of circulation
when Mother Nature freezes us all.
Now there is a day
calling me to action and
I inhale deeply
breathe in the last tendrils
of sunlight as the snow disappears
dripping along the sidewalk
and my heartbeat finds the rhythm
that my shoes are pounding
on the pavement and
just for today
I'm thankful for the weather
and the sunshine and the air
and that indeed I am still able
to do what I do
despite it all
and I am grateful that
this clement day
could be the break
that keeps me going
day after day after
sun-dappled day.

Evening Poem

Inspired by Aaron Davis and his 4 Gs

End of day
Sun is closing her eye
in a palette of corals and golds
soft turquoises and light pinks
Time then
to sit on the patio's picnic table
The one my father built
oh so many years ago
before I was born
now painted a steel blue grey
and drink one last cup of coffee
pensive
not restless
going over the day
the good parts
the things I'm grateful for
the glitch to let go of
the goal for tomorrow
watching colors fade
and the moon awake
with her stars that have been here
oh so many years since
before I was born
appreciating our fleeting impermanence
and the earth's resilience
in this colorful world so vast
it continuously amazes me
on this day now ending

I am humbled to have the experience of it
The picnic table now a shadow underneath me
and coffee cup now empty
the moon guides me inside
to find sleep
hoping for another day

Green Grows Back

Life presents itself in cycles
indifferently.
Where my toes are tickled in hues of green
once was cold barren snow.
A garden, raked and tilled,
now devoid of persecution by the hoe,
will return to lush growth.
In all the painful ways that bare the soil,
give it time,
and green grows back.

Demeter and Persephone

Your ashes will be spread
over the family farm
he said
so that I become Demeter,
goddess of the grain,
and emerge as Persephone.
I shall spring up anew
even after visiting Hades
waiting underground as a seed.
The growing season will return
and I with it
becoming both mother and daughter
celestial and mortal
soil and bud and root and breath
ever cycling
dying, waiting,
regrowing
year after year after
year.

The Robin's Seasons

To everything there is a season — Ecclesiastes 3:1

The robin has returned
singing in trees
and on rooftops
to remind you

there will be a season
where the snow shovel sitting
at the ready on your porch
will be unneeded;
the heavy coats hanging
on the back of your door
out in the open
will seem absurd

there will be a season
to put your flipflops
on the mat in the entryway,
to tug on gardening gloves
or let the soil gather under
your fingernails as you dig
new rows and plant new roots

there will be seasons
to soak in the sun
and dodge raindrops,
to gather snowflakes on tongues
and leaves in piles

there will be a season
to watch trees open and unfurl
while bees scurry to pollinate
neighboring blossoms
around pupae undergoing
their metamorphoses

there will be a season, too
for flying away south,
closing the flowers' blooms,
dropping the leaves
and finding the coats
you shoved into the furthest
closet

There will be a season
of hellos
and a season of
goodbyes,
a season of waking
and a season
to finally
lay down and rest

Acknowledgements

Thank you to so many souls. To my professors, teachers, and mentors, especially the late Bill Kloefkorn, who patiently guided me so my knowledge and poetry could evolve and improve. For my sister and mother, who helped with the nitty gritty details of this book. I love that my mom and I write a poem a week together, using the same prompt: generations of poetry! For my publisher Atmosphere Press, especially Trista Edwards, Ronaldo Alves, and Alex Kale. Gratitude to Marjorie Saiser, Twyla Hansen, Matt Mason, and Bonnie Johnson-Bartee for their support of my writing. For my son and daughter, my inspiration for continuing day to day. For my coworkers, friends, and family for supporting me along the way… this book has been a dream for many years, and now, finally, a reality. Bless you all; I know I could never name everyone.

The following poems have been published before:

'68 International; published May 28, 2019. https://medium.
com/@jpaschold/68-international-ae0f7677eaa9

Arbor Day; published May 8, 2021. https://medium.com/@
jpaschold/arbor-day-a-poem-2a7298c1e884

Free; published September 3, 2022. https://medium.com/the-
power-of-poetry/free-a-poem-f393a6467e1e

Tansy Season; published May 4, 2020. https://jpaschold.blogspot.
com/2020/05/tansy-season-poem.html
Source for definition of *tansy: Webster's Ninth New Collegiate
Dictionary*, Merriam-Webster, Inc. Springfield, Massachusetts
1991 and dictionary.com

Fighting COVID; published Aug 15, 2022. https://medium.com/
the-power-of-poetry/fighting-covid-a-poem-a82cb93f7ed7

Off There; *The Awakenings Review* Volume 6, Number 2. Fall 2015.
The Awakenings Project, Wheaton, IL.

Cowboy Trail, early evening; published April 2, 2020. https://
jpaschold.blogspot.com/2020/04/cowboy-trail-early-evening-
poem.html

Goodbye; *Iconoclast Literary Magazine* #124, 30th Anniversary Edition. Spring 2022. www.iconoclastliterarymagazine.com.

Morning; published September 4, 2020. https://medium.com/ @jpaschold/morning-a-poem-45c2dcadf89

The Supervisor's False Predator; Nebraska Writer's Guild *Stories From the Heartland* (Voices From the Plains Volume 5). 2021. NWG Publications, Scottsbluff, NE.

The Personality of Trees; *Fine Lines* Volume 21, Issue 4. Winter 2012/2013. WriteLife, LLC, Omaha, NE.

Moving Diana; *Fine Lines* Volume 23, Issue 2. Summer 2013. WriteLife, LLC, Omaha, NE.

Evening Poem; published May 6, 2022. https://pensivejournal. com/poetry/evening-poem/.
Inspiration for this poem came from my friend Aaron Davis: https://www.aarondavis.co/about

Information about soils was retrieved from my two agronomy degrees obtained from the University of Nebraska at Lincoln and the following sources:

Agronomy 477/877: Great Plains Field Pedology by David T Lewis. 1997. University of Nebraska Press, Lincoln, NE.

Soils in Our Environment: Seventh Edition by Raymond W. Miller & Roy L. Donahue. 1995. Prentice Hall, Englewood Cliffs, NJ.

A New Definition of Soil by Harold van Es. CSA News, October 2017. American Society of Agronomy, Crop Science Society of America, and Soil Science Society of America.

Author photo by Halla J. Paschold.

About Atmosphere Press

Founded in 2015, Atmosphere Press was built on the principles of Honesty, Transparency, Professionalism, Kindness, and Making Your Book Awesome. As an ethical and author-friendly hybrid press, we stay true to that founding mission today.

If you're a reader, enter our giveaway for a free book here:

SCAN TO ENTER
BOOK GIVEAWAY

If you're a writer, submit your manuscript for consideration here:

SCAN TO SUBMIT
MANUSCRIPT

And always feel free to visit Atmosphere Press and our authors online at atmospherepress.com. See you there soon!

About the Author

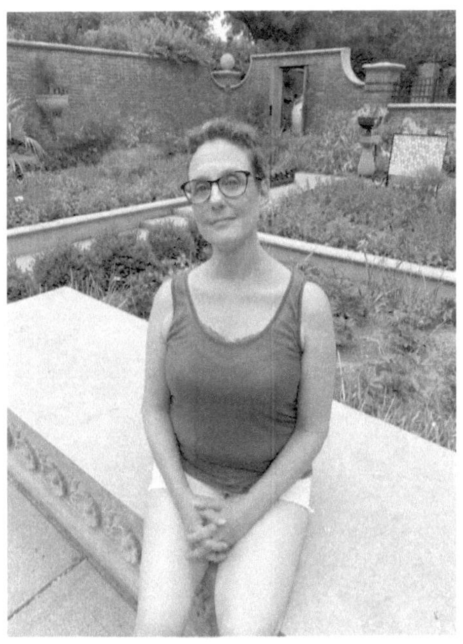 **Julie S. Paschold (Tansy Julie the Soaring Eagle)** is a queer disabled poet and artist from Nebraska. They have their BS and MS in agronomy from the University of Nebraska at Lincoln. Julie has been published in AKA's *Advocate, Fine Lines, Plainsongs, The Awakenings Review,* the Nebraska Writer's Guild, *The Raven's Perch, Iconoclast, The Radical Teacher,* and several publications on medium.com. Two of their chapbooks won honorable mention in contests by Writer's Digest in 2021 and 2022. Julie sells their sketches at Ravenwood in Norfolk, NE. For more, read https://medium.com/@jpaschold or https://jpaschold.blogspot.com/.

www.ingramcontent.com/pod-product-compliance
Lightning Source LLC
Chambersburg PA
CBHW021405150726

47989CB00005B/2405